NATIONAL DEFENSE UNIVERSITY

JOINT FORCES STAFF COLLEGE

JOINT ADVANCED WARFIGHTING SCHOOL

COUNTERINSURGENCY: A FORGOTTEN U.S. STRATEGY

by

Vincent Scott King

LCDR, United States Navy

ABSTRACT

The United States has a history of conducting large, conventional, firepower centric wars to achieve victory. This tactic hindered the U.S. approach to counterinsurgency (COIN) since Vietnam. The U.S. consistently failed to recognize it was fighting an insurgency and instead tried to fight the American Way of War.

The inability of the military to recognize an insurgency and provide a consolidated, comprehensive, and coherent COIN strategy began in the 1960s and continued through today. This inability has proven to be a significant failure for U.S. strategic interests around the world. From Vietnam until today, the U.S. has failed to learn the essential lesson: large, conventional units cannot do nation building or COIN operations due to their size, their inability to conduct de-centralized operations, and their reliance on heavy firepower.

This thesis will examine how U.S. COIN doctrine evolved since Vietnam through a review of historical COIN trends from which U.S. COIN strategy was developed before Vietnam, revised during the interwar years, and reinvented for Iraq, and Afghanistan. This thesis will demonstrate that U.S. doctrine does not show how to link the tactical to strategic applications of COIN properly for success. It then makes recommendations for the future of U.S. counterinsurgency operations.

TABLE OF CONTENTS

CHAPTER 1

Introduction

The Department of Defense created the current counterinsurgency (COIN) doctrine as a result of the stark realization that the U.S. could neither win nor successfully withdraw from Iraq or Afghanistan unless it first recognized what type of war it was engaged in. The type of struggle the United States found itself engaged in was a combination of insurrectionist violence and insurgency. The United States went to war in Iraq and Afghanistan with the most capable and technologically advanced military in world history, but was ill prepared for the violence that ensued once the U.S. achieved its initial military objectives. The military was unable to recognize or even admit that it had entered a quasi-COIN struggle. The military did not know how to plan, direct, or resource a COIN campaign that properly linked the tactical, operational, and strategic applications of a comprehensive and coherent COIN strategy. The failure to address the conditions that defined the operational and strategic environment is revealed in the following conversation between General George Casey, the newly appointed MNF-I commander, and his staff during their first meeting in 2004:

> "Okay who's my counterinsurgency expert," asked General George Casey, sounding impatient. It was his first day in command and his first meeting with the staff he had inherited from General Sanchez, who had left Iraq for good that morning. A dozen Army, Navy, Air Force, and Marine officers sent to Iraq from posts around the world stared at him, stumped by his question. Finally Air Force Major General Steve Sargent spoke up. He had spent his career flying jets, an experience that was largely irrelevant to a fight against low-tech guerillas. "I guess that must be me, sir," said the general, who was in charge of strategic plans at headquarters. The Air Force officer's hesitant answer drove home to Casey how little progress

the military had made during its first year in coming to grips with the kind of war it was fighting.[1]

This inability of the military to recognize an insurgency and provide a consolidated, comprehensive, and coherent COIN strategy began in the 1960s and continued through today. This inability has proven to be a significant failure for U.S. strategic interests around the world. From Vietnam until today, the U.S. has failed to learn the essential lesson: large, conventional units cannot do nation building or COIN operations due to their size, their inability to conduct de-centralized operations, and their reliance on heavy firepower.

Beginning with the Philippine insurrection in 1899 and continuing with Marine Corps operations in Central America and the Caribbean in the early twentieth century, the United States military conducted very low-level quasi-COIN operations often with positive and successful results. In 1940, the Marine Corps collected this knowledge in the *Small Wars Manual* as it revealed truths about the military and unconventional war and provided an insight that the "American soldier had proven as capable as any in adapting to the rigors of unconventional warfare."[2] However, this newly revealed insight was quickly forgotten after Pearl Harbor. Although at least one part of the U.S. military was on the right path to establishing COIN best practices and demonstrating the ability to adapt to unconventional warfare, the onset of World War II changed the focus. As one analyst observed, "the way in which the U.S. fought World War II shaped its character to the present. The approach it took to fighting and winning global conventional war

---

[1] Greg Jaffe and David Cloud, *The Fourth Star* (New York: Crown, 2009), 161.
[2] Thomas R. Mockaitis, *Iraq and the Challenge of Counterinsurgency* (Westport, CT: Praeger Security International, 2008), 34-35.

ultimately inhibited its ability to conduct COIN operations."[3] This large, conventional, and firepower reliant military approach taken by the United States greatly changed the way it thought about, planned, and conducted war. This viewpoint shaped the next 70 years of U.S. military operations. The conventional military leadership in the Cold War had little use for COIN, relegating it to Special Operations Forces (SOF). In both the Vietnam War and in operations in Iraq and Afghanistan, conventional commanders struggled to make sense of factors and conditions that defined insurgency.

This thesis posits that a historical review of U.S. COIN doctrine from the 1960s until today will reveal that a COIN strategy must link tactical, operational, and strategic applications coherently and effectively. From this analysis, some recommendations emerge for revising current COIN doctrine to meet future contingencies.

This thesis will examine how U.S. COIN doctrine evolved since Vietnam to the present through the review of historical COIN vignettes from which much of U.S. COIN strategy was developed. This thesis will demonstrate that U.S. doctrine does not show an understanding of how to link the tactical to strategic applications of COIN properly for success. The future of U.S. counterinsurgency operations will depend on this understanding in order to design a COIN operational approach.

Chapter Two will lay the foundation for understanding COIN by outlining key terminology and definitions associated with insurgency and counterinsurgency and review the origination of the U.S. key COIN concepts and strategies. It will also introduce the first two U.S. Army publications on COIN: FM 31-22, released in 1963

---

[3] Ibib., 35.

and used during the Vietnam War; and FM 3-24, released in 2006 and heralded as the answer to the dilemma of Iraq and Afghanistan.

Chapter Three will provide an examination of the historical COIN operation of the British during the Malayan Emergency that will explain how the U.S. began to think about insurgency and counterinsurgency. It will examine the British approach to COIN and its influence on U.S. COIN concepts. It will also introduce the theorists who became the COIN experts influencing modern doctrine. This case study will serve as an example of the proper application of a COIN strategy.

Chapter Four will examine the U.S. COIN strategy and its applications during the Vietnam War. Beginning with the review of the COIN concepts the United States developed prior to Vietnam, it will establish the fact that the United States understood COIN and applied its concepts correctly. A review of U.S. COIN programs in Vietnam follows, examining the agencies and military forces that conducted COIN, and the successes and failures of these programs. The chapter will evaluate the U.S. strategic approaches of Generals Westmoreland and Abrams and assess the effects of not applying a proper COIN strategy into the overall campaign plan in Vietnam.

Chapter Five will examine the interwar years from 1975 until September 11, 2001. It will examine U.S. involvement in El Salvador and the approach taken to address the insurgency. Counterinsurgency is largely rejected and the military created euphuisms to avoid its unpleasant connotations. It became known as Foreign Internal Defense, and Military Operations Other Than War-tasks for smaller and more specialized forces. Ironically, to allow big units to retain a big war focus. It was very successful due to the nature of small, specialized, and de-centralized units working with the local populace in order to establish security, applying the proper balance of tactical, operational, and strategic approaches essential to a COIN strategy.

Chapter Six will examine the Iraq War and the rediscovery of COIN with the implementation of FM 3-24. Although hailed as the solution, the new doctrine misapplied the wrong lessons of COIN theorists, and ignored the essential linkages that support successful COIN operations.

Chapter Seven will examine the U.S. approach to COIN in the Afghanistan war. It will review the insurgency, provide examples of previously attempted COIN tactics and approaches, and finally, it will examine the most current approach to COIN and introduce its newest initiative to establish Village Stability Operations and the formation of the Afghan local police. It is through the implementation of these two new programs the United States has finally been able to properly link the tactical and operational effects to strategic applications of COIN for success, therefore validating the small unit approach contained in the pre-1940 concepts of the U.S. Marines and the Kitson methodology.

The final chapter will make recommendations for future U.S. COIN operations by presenting an outline of the essential precepts that must be included in future U.S. COIN doctrine.

CHAPTER 2

Introduction

This chapter serves to define key terms and definitions used throughout this thesis. It is imperative to understand these terms and what they actually mean in order to truly comprehend the concept of Counterinsurgency (COIN). These key terms are defined using U.S. Army Field Manuals (FM) and U.S. Joint Publications (JP).

Insurgency

The basis for all discussion in regard to COIN rests in an understanding of what actually constitutes an insurgency. In order to design a proper COIN strategy, one must realize that no two insurgencies are the same. COIN expert Sir Frank Kitson observed, "if you had eighty insurgencies, there were eighty different ways to defeat them."[1]

According to *Counterinsurgency Operations*, Joint Publication 3-24, insurgency is currently defined as "the organized use of subversion or violence by a group or movement that seeks to overthrow or force change of a governing authority."[2] The definition used during and after Vietnam defines insurgency as "an organized, armed political struggle whose goal may be the seizure of power through revolutionary takeover and replacement of the existing government."[3] These definitions only differ slightly with the key difference being the word "subversion or violence" vice "armed." This greatly affects how the U.S. viewed the insurgency and how it would shape U.S. COIN strategy during the Vietnam War. This early definition grew out of President Kennedy's speech

---

[1] Alexander Alderson, "Britain," in *Understanding Counterinsurgency: Doctrine, operations and challenges,* ed. Thomas Rid and Thomas Keaney (New York: Routledge, 2010), 30.

[2] U.S. Joint Chiefs of Staff, *Counterinsurgency Operations*, Joint Publication 3-24 (Washington DC: Joint Chiefs of Staff, October 05 2009), 28.

[3] Steven Metz, "Rethinking Insurgency," in *The Routledge Handbook of Insurgency and Counterinsurgency,* ed. Paul B. Rich and Isabelle Duyvesteyn (New York: Routledge, 2012), 36.

at the 1962 West Point commencement where he described, "another type of war, new in its intensity, ancient in its origins war by guerillas, subversives, insurgents, assassins, war by ambush instead of combat; by infiltration instead of aggression, seeking victory by eroding and exhausting the enemy instead of engaging him."[4] This new type of warfare would be different than what the U.S. military had trained for or was built to fight.

Although no two insurgencies are the same, there are some basic characteristics that all insurgencies share and must be considered and examined in order to understand the conditions that define an insurgency.

[5]

These characteristics must be understood based on the enemy one is fighting at a certain time and place. They are a starting point from which to understand who and what you are facing, and are used as the basis for beginning to analyze and implement a COIN strategy. They must be reevaluated throughout the planning and implementation of a COIN strategy because they will shift constantly.

---

[4] Ibid., 35.
[5] U.S. Joint Chiefs of Staff, *Counterinsurgency Operations,* JP 3-24, 46.

In addition to the characterstics of an insurgency, there are eight dynamics of an insurgency that can be used to assess the strengths and weaknesses of the enemy.

These dynamics are all interactive and vital to understanding how to defeat an insurgency. The U.S. has displayed an inability during COIN operations to understand the core characteristics and dynamics of insurgency leading to the desire to use a large conventional force that was inadequately trained and resourced to conduct COIN operations. The U.S. has been unsuccessful in defeating insurgencies as a result.

Counterinsurgency (COIN)

The key to developing and implementing a COIN strategy is first understanding the insurgency at hand and secondly, understanding how to counter it. The definition of COIN from FM 31-22, the U.S forces used during Vietnam was "military, paramilitary, political, economic, psychological, and civic actions taken by a government to defeat a subversive insurgency."[7] The modern definition used today is from JP 3-24, which states "comprehensive civilian and military efforts to defeat an insurgency and to address any core grievances."[8] These definitions are useful in defining COIN but do not provide any

---

[6] Ibid., 52.
[7] Headquarters Department of the Army, *U.S. Army Counterinsurgency Forces FM 31-22,* Department of the Army, (Washington D.C., 1963), 5.
[8] U.S. Joint Chiefs of Staff, *Counterinsurgency Operations,* JP 3-24, 28.

help in the development of a successful strategy or how to begin addressing an insurgency.

The first and most important step in developing an effective COIN strategy is knowing that an insurgency exists and knowing the nature of the insurgency. The next step is the establishment of security and support for the population within the parameters of their culture. The interaction with people through numerous approaches involving not just military force is crucial in COIN. As previously discussed, the U.S. conducted COIN operations in the early 20th century that produced the desired results. Forces conducting COIN operations understood what was required in this type of warfare as shown in this quote from the *Small Wars Manual*:

> In small wars, caution must be exercised, and instead of striving to generate the maximum power with forces available, the goal is to gain decisive results with the least application of force. In small wars, tolerance, sympathy, and kindness should be the keynote of our relationship with the mass of the population. Small wars involve a wide range of activities including diplomacy, contacts with the civilian population and warfare of the most difficult kind.[9]

This understanding of COIN gave way to a large, conventional military mindset and forced the U.S. to continuously search for an effective counterinsurgency strategy. The U.S. approach to implementing COIN doctrine since Vietnam has been a very "cookie cutter" approach combined with a "this looks good, let's try it and a one size fits all" approach. There was never any thought put into designing a successful COIN strategy to nest in the overall U.S. campaign strategy used during Vietnam, Iraq, and the early years of Afghanistan. Published in December 2006, the Department of Defense saw FM 3-24 as the new answer for the U.S. when it came to COIN. However, it falls short because its theoretical based, historical lessons approach does little to address how

---

[9] Ibid., 74.

to conduct a COIN campaign and properly link tactical success to strategic objectives for an overall COIN strategy.

Unconventional Warfare

Unconventional Warfare (UW) is a core mission set of Special Operations Forces (SOF) that JP 3-05 defines as "those activities conducted to enable a resistance movement or insurgency to coerce, disrupt, or overthrow a government or occupying power by operating through or with an underground, auxiliary, and guerilla force in a denied area."[10] This thesis will discuss the United States effort in El Salvador in a later chapter. The El Salvador conflict is an example of how the U.S. relegated COIN to SOF because COIN was seen as an outlying nuisance vice a type of warfare the military should train or plan for.

Foreign Internal Defense

Foreign Internal Defense (FID) is another SOF core mission set that JP 3-05 defines as "U.S. activities that support a host nation's internal defense and development strategy designed to protect against subversion, lawlessness, insurgency, terrorism, and other threats to their security, stability, and legitimacy."[11] Conventional and Special Operations Forces conduct FID through Theater Security Cooperation Plan events designed to train, advise, assist, and evaluate host nation forces during peacetime in order to ensure that they can maintain peace and stability in their country and to prepare them as allies to be called upon during conflict. The following chart shows the characteristics of FID. These characteristics are the building blocks upon which the U.S. builds foreign

---

[10] U.S. Joint Chiefs of Staff, *Special Operations*, Joint Publication 3-05 (Washington DC: Joint Chiefs of Staff, April 18 2011), 32.
[11] Ibid., 34.

partnerships and influence around the globe.

12

FID is a key peacetime strategy that the U.S. uses to ensure its overall engagement strategy is focused on collective security.

Stability Operations

JP 3-0 defines Stability Operations as an "overarching term encompassing various military missions, tasks, and activities conducted outside the United States in coordination with other instruments of national power to maintain or reestablish a safe and secure environment, provide essential governmental services, emergency infrastructure reconstruction, and humanitarian relief."[13] These types of operations have come to the forefront of the U.S. military during both the Iraq and Afghanistan Wars. The U.S. conducts stability ops before, during, and after combat operations. After 12 years of security, stability, transition, and recovery operations in both Iraq and Afghanistan, the U.S. military is no longer shaping the Joint Force 2020 to conduct these types of operations due to the fiscally constrained environment and the proposed downsizing of the force. The U.S. will be forced to use the military in concert with all elements of national power in order to achieve success in future stability operations.

---

[12] U.S. Joint Chiefs of Staff, *Special Operations*, JP 3-05, 34.

[13] U.S. Joint Chiefs of Staff, *Joint Operations*, Joint Publication 3-0 (Washington DC: Joint Chiefs of Staff, August 11 2011), 200.

11

Guerilla Warfare

JP 1-02 defines Guerilla Warfare (GW) as "Military and paramilitary operations conducted in enemy-held or hostile territory by irregular, predominantly indigenous forces."[14] Initial U.S. involvement in Vietnam was centered on countering GW. This thesis discusses this in a later chapter in concert with the initial strategy used to deal with the insurgency in Vietnam.

Conclusion

This chapter served to introduce the reader to all applicable terms used throughout this thesis. The following chapter provides an examination of the British COIN struggle in Malaya. This case study serves as an example of a successful COIN campaign upon which the U.S. attempted to base its COIN philosophy.

---

[14] U.S. Joint Chiefs of Staff, *Department of Defense Dictionary of Military and Associated Terms,* Joint Publication 1-02 (Washington DC: Joint Chiefs of Staff, October 15 2013), 123.

CHAPTER 3

Introduction

The Malayan Emergency lasted from 1948 until 1960 and is considered by many as one of the most successful counterinsurgency (COIN) campaigns to date. It serves as the basis and example for much of the current United States COIN doctrine. This chapter will examine the British approach to COIN in Malaya. It will begin with a background of the Malayan Emergency, discuss the approach employed by the British and how this approach was successful at linking the tactical and operational to the strategic applications of COIN for success, and will introduce some key COIN theorists that emerge from this campaign and will heavily influence the way COIN is understood by many practitioners.

Background

The British association began in Malaya in 1786 and continued to grow until 1914 when all of the Malayan states finally began to accept the advice of Edward Lewis Brockman, the British Chief Secretary of the Federations, and other British residents' advice on all Malayan colonial matters other than religion. The tin mining and rubber planting industries increased during British expansion as Malayan exports rose in world importance. This growth of industry and the need for a more experienced work force led to the migration of Chinese laborers.

In the 1920's, the Chinese labor force and mine owners established a network of Secret Societies in Malaya that the British-run government broke up giving way to Kuomintang influenced Chinese communities. The Malayan Communist Party (MCP) formed in 1930 due to the split between the Kuomintang and Chinese communists. The outbreak of World War II and subsequent occupation of Malaya by Japan led to the establishment of the Malayan Peoples Anti-Japanese Army (MPAJA), a guerilla force formed from the MCP and trained by the British after the Japanese conquest of Malaya in 1942. At the end of World War II, the MCP planned to take control of Malaya but the sudden ending found the MCP not ready to assume control. Therefore, the British maintained control of Malaya.

The British establishment of the Federation of Malaya shortly after World War II led to the starting point for the insurgency because of the ethnic tensions created between the Malays and Chinese. As the MCP gained influence and infiltrated urban organizations in their new urban approach, their rural communist base began to decline. This base is what they had come to depend on during WW II and existed at the jungles edge. It would soon come back to the forefront and serve as the new launching point for the insurgency. In May 1948, the MCP decided to launch a full scale insurgency in order to seize control of Malaya. The insurgency emerged out of "a communist party fueled by the frustration of internal strife, angered by racial inequalities, and spurred by ideological fervor." [1] Chin Peng led this insurgency after he assumed control when the former Secretary General of the MCP stole all of the MCP funds. Chin Peng quickly mobilized 3,000 guerilla jungle fighters that would become the Malayan Peoples Anti-British Army (MPBBA) and 7,000 part-time guerillas known as the Self Protection Corps.

In June of 1948 the British Government in Malaya declared a State of Emergency and in July they declared the MCP illegal. "By the end of the year over 2,000 people had

---

[1] Andrew Mumford, *The Counter-Insurgency Myth: The British Experience of Irregular Warfare* (New York: Routledge, 2012), 27.

been either detained or deported, and Chin Peng acknowledged the fact that it would be necessary to settle down to a long drawn out war."[2] This acknowledgement by Chin Peng ultimately ensured the foundation for a counterinsurgency that lasted for many years. He immediately renamed the MPBBA to the Malayan Races Liberation Army (MRLA) and reorganized his organization to establish a political base among the population. The MRLA began their campaign to resist colonial capitalist interests, workers, and British security forces. As a result of this and a call by ex-patriots for more help in the insurgency, the British appointed Lieutenant General Sir Harold Briggs as the Director of Operations.

British COIN Approach

The introduction of the Federation Plan for the Elimination of the Communist Organization and Armed Forces in Malaya became as the "Briggs Plan" and was the foundation upon which the British built their COIN strategy. Introduced in July 1950, the four stated goals of the Briggs Plan were:

(1) clearing the country of guerillas methodically from south to north
(2) resettling the numerous Chinese squatters, the principal source of food for the guerillas, into secured villages
(3) uprooting the guerilla infrastructure inside the cleared areas and
(4) closely coordinating civil and military activities[3]

Briggs introduced this plan and implemented it with some success. However, it gained momentum Sir Gerald Templer was appointed both the High Commissioner and Director of Operations in February 1952. He understood the key role of good intelligence in COIN operations and used it as the basis for how to fight the insurgency. Templer was responsible for shifting away from the "search and destroy" mindset of

---

[2] Frank Kitson, *Bunch of Five* (London: Faber & Faber, 1977), 73.
[3] Anthony James Joes, *Guerilla Warfare* (Westport, CT: Greenwood Press, 1996), 85.

COIN to the "hearts and minds" approach to defeat the insurgency. Templer believed "the answer [to the terrorists] lies not in pouring more soldiers into the jungle, but rests in the hearts and minds of the people."[4] His new approach was the catalyst for success in Malaya.

Contributing Success Factors

The largest single contributing factor to the success of the British COIN strategy was the resettlement of the Chinese squatters into new villages. These squatters received title to their new lands, and in addition to the food control and denial programs instituted by the British, slowly denied the insurgents their main pool of dissatisfied people from which to build and supply their insurgent fighting force. These programs were "the most effective planned operation against a guerilla force and its support organizations …. It was a devastating measure that did more than any other single thing to defeat the Communists in Malaya."[5]

In addition to the resettlement program, the British employed professional jungle fighters to penetrate the guerilla safe havens. These fighters destroyed food supplies, intercepted and interrupted messenger systems, deprived the insurgents of sleep, and kept them on the move and unable to anticipate or plan large scale operations.[6] These jungle fighters, which became the Malayan Scouts, were the precursor to the modern day British Special Air Service that developed from the original idea by Major Michael "Mad Mike" Calvert.

---

[4] Dr. Paul Melshen, "The Malayan Emergency" (lecture, Joint Forces Staff College, Norfolk, VA, November 6, 2013).
[5] Joes, *Guerilla Warfare*, 85.
[6] Ibid., 86.

Another key strategy employed by Templer was the marginalization of the insurgent's political focus on Chinese-Malay ethnic tensions. He granted citizenship to Malayan born Chinese and formed a home guard as a local militia. Through his civil strategy of joining the Malayans and Chinese, he eventually convinced the Malayan and Chinese to form an alliance. This political alliance would eventually seal the fate of the insurgency by demonstrating that change could come without the Communist insurgency.

The other key contributing factor to the success in Malaya was the increase in British regular troops and establishment of Malayan security forces. In addition to the increase in security, intelligence was seen as a key to success in Malaya. As previously mentioned, Templer understood the importance that intelligence played in defeating a COIN. He established the Special Branch in order to gain intelligence from a network of informers, agents, and turned prisoners. This effort played a key role in finding the insurgents and ultimately defeating them.

The main reason Templer was able to fully implement the Briggs Plan with some of his own adaptations was because the British appointed him the High Commissioner and the Director of Operations. His unique position gave him the authority as the chief civil and military commander to make all decisions surrounding the fight against the insurgents and he made it clear that everything else in Malaya was subordinate to the task of defeating the Communists. The real success in Malaya lay in the foundational principles of the Briggs Plan carried out through the leadership, and unique command and control structure which Templer enjoyed as the primary decision maker in Malaya.

The British success in Malaya was largely due to the early establishment of the Briggs Plan because it served as the basis of the COIN strategy carried out by Templer.

All of these " converging programs---resettlement and food denial, uprooting the insurgent infrastructure, clear moves toward independence, high rewards for good information, penetration of the jungle, reliance on numbers rather than firepower, coordination of effort---eventually had a devastating effect on the guerillas." [7] The Emergency officially ended on July 31, 1960. Malaya was touted as the premier example of what a COIN strategy should look like.

Contributing Circumstances

Although considered a very successful COIN campaign, there were other circumstances one must consider when discussing how successful the British were in Malaya. These circumstances helped allow for success and, without them, the Emergency may have turned out differently. These circumstances include the following: very little outside support or assistance from Communist nations; no sanctuary for the Malayan guerillas due to the isolation on three sides from the British navy and the support of Thailand to the British cause; the inability of the insurgents to employ the nationalism cause because the British had already identified this issue in their plan and were moving towards independence for Malaya; the inability of the insurgency to reach out to other ethnic groups and get them to join the insurgency vice just the Chinese minority of Malaya conducting the insurgency; the inability of the insurgents to develop a response to the resettlement program, which decisively separated them from their supporters; and the relative smallness of Malaya which made it easier to isolate the country and supervise the population. These circumstances were all in the favor of the British and allowed them to effectively and systematically defeat the insurgency.[8]

---

[7] Joes, *Guerilla Warfare*, 86.
[8] Ibid., 87.

Emerging COIN Theorists and Experts

During the Malayan Emergency, many British COIN experts contributed to their successful strategy and they went on to greatly influence how the United States viewed COIN. The writings of these men and the historical lessons from Malaya were studied in great detail during the development of FM 3-24, the current United States Army guide on COIN. Sir Robert Thompson, who served in Malaya as a staff member on the British Director of Operations under Lieutenant General Sir Harry Briggs and General Sir Gerald Templer wrote an influential book, *Defeating Communist Insurgency: The Lessons of Malaya and Vietnam* that serves as a reference within FM 3-24. Sir Thompson also served as the leader of the British Advisory Mission to South Vietnam and advised President Nixon.

Another contributor to COIN strategy that emerged from Malaya was Sir Frank Kitson. He served in Kenya during the Mau Mau uprising and went on to write numerous books on COIN and low intensity operations. He understood that no two insurgencies are the same, and that it takes proper coordination at all levels throughout both civil and military organizations for a COIN strategy to succeed.

Sir Gerald Templer is known for his implementation of the Briggs Plan and the successful defeat of the Communist insurgency in Malaya. However, his most famous contribution was his 'Hearts and Minds' quote that was copied and used by numerous United States presidents, generals, and even in the current FM 3-24 manual. Despite this quote serving as the bumper sticker for the Vietnam War, the sad fact is the United States had no idea what Templer actually meant by the quote and had no idea how to implement it for success in Vietnam.

Conclusion

The Malayan Emergency is seen as the example to follow in order to implement a successful COIN strategy. The key to implementing a successful COIN strategy is firstly the realization that you are fighting an insurgency and secondly the need to build a comprehensive strategy that successfully links the tactical, operational, and strategic applications of COIN for success. This realization and successful strategy in Malaya is readily apparent throughout this chapter. It is also evident in this quote from Sir Frank Kitson:

> there can be no such thing as a purely military solution because insurgency is not primarily a military activity. At the same time there is no such thing as a wholly political solution either, short of surrender, because the very fact that a state of insurgency exists implies that violence is involved which will have to be countered to some extent at least by the use of legal force. Political measures alone might have prevented the insurgency in the first place, . . . [but] once it has taken hold, politics and force, backed by economic measures will have to be harnessed together for the purpose of restoring peaceful conditions. [9]

The British were able to defeat the Communist insurgency because they realized it takes a combination of both civil and military actions, along with the building of internal security forces, in order to meet the first and most basic tenet of COIN which is protection and security of the population.

This chapter introduced the British approach to COIN through the review of the Malayan Emergency. They were successful in defeating the insurgency because of their ability to create a comprehensive and coherent strategy that was properly applied and understood throughout all levels of military and civilian leadership, and their ability to

---

[9] Alderson, "Britain," in *Understanding Counterinsurgency: Doctrine, operations, and challenges*, 30.

link the tactical and operational to strategic applications of COIN for success. The Malaya Emergency served as an example for the United States to follow when it came to establishing a COIN strategy during the Vietnam War. However, the inability of the United States military leadership to realize the type of war it was fighting, construct and implement a COIN strategy, apply the properly trained forces to carry out the strategy, and apply lessons learned from Malaya would cause the war to last much longer than necessary. The following chapter examines these factors and the overall attitude and approach by the military leaders in Vietnam.

CHAPTER 4

Introduction

The United States entered the Vietnam War with an understanding of how to implement a counterinsurgency (COIN) strategy. The real question was would the U.S. be able to take the lessons of past COIN struggles and successfully apply them to the current struggle? The biggest problem facing military leaders was that they focused and centered on conventional war instead of COIN. This chapter examines the U.S. COIN strategy in Vietnam and its application. It will examine a previous U.S. COIN campaign that proved successful, highlight some early programs that were both successful and unsuccessful, and review the U.S. approach to the Vietnam War through both doctrine and the strategic approach of two commanding generals.

Historical Success

The Huk rebellion in the Philippines is as an example of a successful COIN campaign the United States waged at the same time the British were dealing with the Malayan insurgency. Like Malaya, the insurgency grew out of a resistance against the Japanese occupation, and continued after the war as an opposition to the newly formed government. The U.S. was involved from 1946 until the rebellion ended in 1954. This campaign is the first U.S. COIN operation because it highlights the differences from the ideas of conventional combat and the nature of the type of layered approach needed to defeat an insurgency. Although the U.S. never committed forces to combat during the Huk rebellion, the influence of the Joint United States Military Assistance Advisory Group (JUSMAAG) and the role it played during the rebellion were keys to the success. The military technical advice and training from the advisors, as well as military and economic aid, were seen as a way to put a nation on the path to success when dealing with a COIN operation.[1]

U.S. ability to understand COIN grew out of this rebellion. However, still lurking in the background of U.S. military thought was this idea and premise of large, conventional operations that grew out of WW II. This idea was ingrained in U.S. military thought and seen as the way to wage war. One historian has observed that "many MAAG officers felt that [unconventional] techniques violated the military managerial and tactical principles that had won World War II in the forties and were surely applicable to revolutionary conflicts in the fifties."[2] This adversity to unconventional techniques would ultimately hamper the U.S. ability to wage and win the war in Vietnam.

Early Programs

Strategic Hamlet Program

This program grew out of the British experience in Malaya and followed along the lines of their resettlement program. Sir Robert Thompson, who served in Malaya and saw this successful program, advocated for the use of what was called the 'oil spot' strategy. This well-known approach to COIN originated with the Frenchman Joseph Gallieni during his days of quelling rebellions in both French Sudan and Indochina. This heavily influenced the French approach to COIN and, in turn, some of its ideas found their way into FM 3-24 in 2006 through the study of David Galula.

The Strategic Hamlet program was doomed from the start due to the fact that the Diem government of South Vietnam ignored Thompson's input and built the first hamlets deep inside areas dominated by the Viet Cong (VC). Along with location, the lack of

---

[1] Douglas S. Blaufarb, *The Counterinsurgency Era: U.S. Doctrine and Performance, 1950 to the Present* (New York: The Free Press, 1977), 40.
[2] Ibid., 38.

village autonomy, requirement to build your own hamlet, and the forcing of rural people to abandon their way of life for security caused this strategy to be unsuccessful. The largest contributing factor to this unsuccessful program was the ability of the VC to attack these hamlets and the will of the regular South Vietnamese troops. By the end of 1964, the VC had overrun all of the showcase hamlets causing the South Vietnamese to cancel the program.

Civilian Irregular Defense Groups (CIDG)

CIDG was a program that started in the central highlands of South Vietnam's western border area with the local people called Montagnards. It began in November 1961 with the arrival of 24 U.S. Army Green Berets under the direction of the CIA. This was a guerilla warfare type operation designed to organize and train a paramilitary unit that could provide village security, and possibly create a force to conduct selective offensive operations and border surveillance. Upon showing initial success, more training teams arrived and the program started to gain momentum. However, the U.S. Army senior leadership did not agree with the CIDG being under CIA control and had all authorities shifted to military control. This is when the CIDG program began to shift focus from mutually supporting village based security networks to regional militia forces. The U.S. relocated these forces to block infiltration routes from Cambodia.

The Strategic Hamlet program's mistake was again repeated in the CIDG program with the shift of peoples to locations outside of their areas of influence and security. In addition, they had the same issues with the VC attacking these new camp areas as well as problems that arose out of the relationship between the South Vietnamese Special Forces and the CIDG camps and forces.

The decision by General Westmoreland to shift the CIDG authorities to military control ultimately doomed this tactically successful program that could have possibly led to strategic gains and effects. The conventional mindset of the U.S. military leaders eclipsed any true appreciation of developing a COIN strategy for Vietnam. This mindset is evident in the following passage:

> The evolution of the Special Forces program from local defense to offensive combat operations was another recurring theme of American counterinsurgency efforts. American officers . . . . were imbued with an aggressive military philosophy summarized in the phrase "find 'em, fix 'em, destroy 'em." In their experience American mobility and firepower reigned supreme. They deemed the slow business of pacification unpalatable and did not think that it should tie down American fighting men.[3]

This fixation with offensive maneuver warfare would lead to the introduction of brigades and divisions into Vietnam and shift the focus from an unconventional war to a manpower and firepower centric war.

General Westmoreland's Approach

American political and military leadership did not see the conflict in Vietnam going the way the way they wanted it to go. The U.S. grew impatient with the South Vietnamese and their inability to stem the tide of the VC creating the decision to increase U.S. military involvement. In June 1964, the U.S. decided to transition from an advisory mission under Military Assistance Advisory Group (MAAG), through assistance with the Military Assistance Command Vietnam (MACV), to a consolidated American headquarters in Vietnam commanded by General William Westmoreland. Westmoreland

---

[3] James R. Arnold, *Jungle of Snakes* (New York: Bloomsbury Press, 2009), 193-94.

commanded MACV from June 1964 until July 1968, and his ideas of how to win this war would ultimately hamper the COIN effort.

In 1965, with the arrival of conventional U.S. combat forces in Vietnam, the war began to change and take a new shape. There were actually two wars being fought simultaneously, a counterinsurgency and a conventional war. The problem that grew out of fighting two wars was the approach taken to defeat the insurgency. Westmoreland realized the need for COIN but felt the South Vietnamese should conduct it because they understood the language and the culture. He believed that the path to victory was through a war of attrition with Communist regular units using American combat power to bring a swift end as evidenced in this passage:

> the U.S. army acted according to its limited-war doctrine, which called for rapid restoration of peace achieved by decisive combat with the enemy. This doctrine played to the army's strengths: its massive firepower and tremendous mobility. . . . the army would conduct a war of attrition utilizing the weapons and tactics designed to defeat the Soviet Union in a conventional conflict. It would grind down the Communists until they gave up. The "Other War", the counterinsurgency campaign, would always be subordinate to this war of attrition. When asked at a press conference what was the answer to insurgency, Westmoreland gave a one-word reply: "Firepower."[4]

This approach would complicate the COIN effort and, as witnessed above, make it a lesser priority for MACV.

There were, however, some large conventional units having great success in the COIN effort. The Marines had a history of conducting COIN in Central America in the early 1900s, codified in the *Small Wars Manual*, a resource for understanding how to fight an insurgency. The Marine Corps had an assigned area of responsibility consisting

---

[4] Ibid., 218.

of five provinces located in the northernmost region of South Vietnam along the North Vietnamese border. General Lewis Walt, the commander of the Marine Expeditionary Force, quickly realized upon his arrival in Vietnam that a different approach was needed for success in this war and he introduced the Combined Action Program (CAP). This concept was originally devised to defend military installations at Phu Bai airfield from VC attack but quickly became a viable and expandable COIN tactic capable of accomplishing the most basic tenet of COIN-security for the population. This COIN tactic centered around a fourteen man rifle company along with a navy corpsman and a 38-man local militia force. The CAP force's primary objective was the destruction of insurgent infrastructure within villages, and the protection of the people and government officials against reprisal attacks. This approach was very successful tactically, but could not be implemented to any greater extent because there was no strategy to support it. U.S. policy would not accept such a commitment in time or resources.

Contrary to the Marine Corps operations, General Westmoreland settled on three categories of operations in support of his Vietnam strategy: search and destroy, clear and hold, and securing operations. The problem with this strategy was that it placed primary emphasis on search and destroy missions instead of taking into account the paradigm that the insurgent picks the time and place to attack and he knows the terrain much better than you. It also fails to account for the protection of local populations during battles. This killing of locals and the United States' inability to protect them ultimately improved the ability of the insurgents to coerce the local villagers to their side.

While the U.S. strategy recognized it could not win by offensive operations alone and there was a need for pacification, the U.S. did not fully address it until the 1966

Army Staff report entitled, *A Program for the Pacification and Long-Term Development of South Vietnam* (PROVN). The study indicted "the U.S. government for failing to create a unified and well-coordinated program for eliminating the insurgency in South Vietnam. It argued that pacification - establishing control over and winning the support of the population - was the essence of the problem, to which all actions had to be subordinated."[5] Although never fully implemented, PROVN became the model for what the U.S. implemented in 1967 called the Civil Operations and Revolutionary Development Support (CORDS). CORDS was a highly integrated civilian and military structure used to restore the legitimacy of the South Vietnamese government at the village level. The U.S. set up this program to consolidate and coordinate all the disparate civilian and military pacification programs under one directorate.

Over the four years that General Westmoreland was COMMACV, the U.S. military presence grew from 23,000 to 536,000 troops. The approach taken to COIN was haphazard at best and lacked the full backing of the U.S. military leadership. The U.S. dabbled with COIN programs, but never put their full weight behind anything other than victory by attrition and firepower. In 1968, General Creighton Abrams assumed command of MACV. By this time in the war, the U.S. had already committed to withdrawal from Vietnam, and COIN reemerged as the dominant approach to the war. What begin to emerge looked amazingly like some of the programs started 10 years earlier.

---

[5] Andrew J. Birtle, PROVN, "Westmoreland, and the Historians: A Reappraisal," *The Journal of American History* 72, no. 10 (October 2008): 1214, studie .in   PROVN W   and. df (accessed November 20, 2013).

General Abrams Approach

On 1 July 1968, General Abrams assumed command of MACV and designed a new strategy for victory in Vietnam. His new one-war plan emerged out of the convoluted two-war plan embraced by Westmoreland. This new plan relied on South Vietnamese support and set out to adopt an integrated pacification program that recognized the need to keep Communist main-force elements away from population areas and root out VC infrastructure within the south. This new plan began to sound like a COIN strategy the U.S. could implement at the tactical level for growth to the strategic level.

Abrams shifted the strategic focus from large U.S. forces locating and attacking large enemy units to working with regional and local paramilitary forces from the Army of the Republic of Vietnam (ARVN) to conduct small unit operations in populated areas. This new structure closely resembled the British approach in Malaya, where the use of conventional forces in concert with local militia divided the insurgents from the people. This shift in focus helped establish security for the population and as one historian has assessed "by 1970 a considerable measure of security had been restored and the ability of the insurgency to affect events, to mobilize the population, to fight, tax, and recruit had been eroded to the point where it was manageable threat." [6] However, this newly formulated COIN strategy was too little, too late. With the U.S. withdrawing large numbers of troops, Vietnamization and the defense of the Republic of Vietnam from a conventional North Vietnam invasion became the focus of the Thieu government.

---

[6] Blaufarb, *The Counterinsurgency Era*, 270.

Conclusion

Instead of Vietnam being fought as a classic COIN operation, it would be fought as a conventional war. There were some early successful programs such as the CIDG and CAP that could have served as the basis for a COIN strategy. However, U.S. military leadership did not follow through with these programs and it led to Vietnam being becoming a failed COIN campaign. During the war, the U.S. military had opportunities to fight this war differently, using a COIN strategy that followed the British model from Malaya. Instead, it chose to expend resources on the big-unit war, a war of attrition that Westmoreland thought he understood and believed he could win.[7]

The inability of the U.S. to properly link the tactical, operational, and strategic applications of COIN in Vietnam ultimately led to the defeat of U.S. strategic objectives. Tactics and operations were not the problem. The real problem was that the nation building strategy was not compatible with a largely tactical COIN approach. Operationally, COIN was ignored in favor of big unit operations directed at the North Vietnamese army. According to historian Douglas Porch, "The errors were made on a much higher level. The American military seriously underestimated the difficulties involved in dealing with the enemy forces. . . . In short, American leaders, both civilian and military, committed a strategic blunder that has brought many Generals to grief: they chose the wrong battlefield."[8]

Unfortunately, the COIN lessons of Vietnam would quickly fade away and military leadership would relegate that 'dirty word' they call COIN to Special Operations Forces. The U.S. military would experience a significant force reduction during the post-

---

[7] Arnold, *Jungle of Snakes*, 236.
[8] Douglas Porch, *Counterinsurgency: Exposing the Myths of the New Way of War* (New York: Cambridge University Press, 2013), 222.

30

Vietnam years in combination with a resource constrained budget that caused all service components to man, train, and equip for only large, conventional formations. These factors along with the lingering bad taste of the withdrawal from Vietnam only pushed COIN further away from the thinking of the conventional military. The following chapter will look at the interwar years from post-Vietnam until September 11, 2001 when COIN was thrust outside the mainstream of military doctrine. However, this would quickly change in 2004 when COIN became the new focus of the U.S. military.

CHAPTER 5:

Introduction

This chapter examines the United States approach and overall attitude to counterinsurgency (COIN) between post-Vietnam and September 11, 2001. The ideas of insurgency and counterinsurgency that had garnered great interest in the early 1960s came to an abrupt end with the Vietnam War. The lack of successful operational experiences involving COIN greatly influenced future U.S. doctrine as evidenced in the following quote: "In the aftermath of U.S. withdrawal from Vietnam, counterinsurgency was deliberately eliminated from U.S. military doctrine, as the armed forces turned their attention to the Central Front and the prospect of armored confrontation with the Soviet Union."[1] Once again, as in the past, the large conventional military approach dominated the conversation and the U.S. pushed COIN to the backburner.

The neglect of COIN immediately following Vietnam caused a need for rediscovery as the U.S. entered the 1980s and concern grew about Third World instability.[2] As a result of communist inspired revolutionary movements, the Reagan administration developed a strategy for what it called the "rollback of communism." Special Operations Forces were deployed to conduct small advisory type operations to support countries threatened by insurgency. Although largely tactical COIN, it did have a supporting strategy and clearly stated ends. In El Salvador, small units employed for decisive results led to a satisfactory result for U.S. strategic interests. The end of the Cold War gave rise to a new term that began to appear in U.S. doctrine called Foreign

---

[1] David H. Ucko "Whither Counterinsurgency?," in *The Routledge Handbook of Insurgency and Counterinsurgency*, ed. Paul B. Rich and Isabelle Duvyesteyn (New York: Routledge, 2012), 73.
[2] Ibid., 73.

Internal Defense (FID). FID dominated U.S. doctrine in the 1990s as the answer to COIN and remained this way until 2004 when the U.S. required real COIN doctrine to conduct operations in Iraq.

This thesis highlights the struggle in El Salvador in order to demonstrate the U.S. approach to COIN in the post-Vietnam military. El Salvador was one of many hot spots during the Cold War where SOF served as the tactical COIN force operating to support a clearly defined strategic goal. SOF served as the U.S. answer to conducting COIN as the rest of the military concentrated on large conventional battles that never came to fruition.

El Salvador Background

El Salvador is a small Central American country with a history of oligarchical control and military dictatorship where an army of officer elites rule over a conscript army who, in combination with the oligarchy, conducted numerous human rights abuses. The combination of social unrest with the lack of government assistance to the population led to the rise of the Faribundo Marti National Liberation Front (FMLN), a communist-based revolutionary group that sought to replace the ruling party through subversion and military action.

The leadership and organizational abilities of the FMLN posed a challenge to the Salvadoran military and, as a result, the military and police resorted to death squads to keep the rebel forces from gaining popular support and recruits. Despite the reputation of these death squads, the U.S. pledged its support to the government of El Salvador in 1980, in order to, ensure the defeat of the communist-based insurgency and to prevent the further spread of communism in the Western hemisphere. U.S. economic and military aid helped to stabilize the U.S. backed government. Thus, the U.S. strategic goals had a similarity to the British goals in Malaya. Instead of conducting nation building like Vietnam, this strategy was similar to the British and sought to control a communist inspired insurgency from the inside. In 1981, President Reagan sent a small number of SOF advisors into the country and, in 1982 Salvadoran officers began COIN training at Fort Bragg.

U.S. Approach

The U.S. used a tactical COIN approach directly from the *Small Wars Manual*. Indeed, the focus on small units to achieve decisive results, the winning of the population over to the government of El Salvador, and developing a capable indigenous conventional and militia force supported by economic aid, military hardware sales, and limited advisory efforts were all key components of the U.S. approach. Mobile Training Teams were sent to advise, assist, and train Salvadoran forces in infantry, artillery, and intelligence tactics, techniques, and procedures. The U.S. advisors assisted in training local self-defense forces along with the military to help establish the government's legitimacy and provide security to the peasants. Special Operations Forces, along with the Central Intelligence Agency, trained specialized units for long range patrols to track down insurgents, just as the British did in Malaya. The SOF advisory and teaching role that started in Vietnam continued through the Cold War era and gave rise to FID as it is known today. The success of this COIN effort illustrated the traditional tactical focus of U.S. COIN. With strong interagency support backed by a clear strategy-this tactical effort met U.S. strategic goals.

Conclusion

This chapter discussed the U.S. approach to COIN during the interwar years through a review of the struggle of the El Salvadoran government against a communist-based insurgency. Armed with a proper COIN strategy similar to that of the British in Malaya, the U.S. developed an interagency approach with U.S. SOF conducting tactical level COIN using El Salvadoran forces and U.S. resources to isolate the insurgents from the people to promote stability. The new approach to COIN, or FID as it came to be known, relegated these types of operations to SOF. The relegation of COIN to SOF grew out of the failure in Vietnam to apply a COIN strategy for success and the desire to concentrate on conventional vice unconventional warfare. Post-Vietnam U.S. military doctrine reflected this idea as COIN became subsumed into broad task groups such as Low-Intensity Conflict, Military Operations Other Than War, and Stability and Support Operations which were catch-all categories for missions it did not want to perform. This decision would leave the vast majority of regular forces unprepared for the COIN campaign that it faced on the post 9/11 battlefield.[3] The following chapter will examine the Iraq War and the U.S. approach to COIN.

---

[3] Thomas R. Mockaitis, *Resolving Insurgencies* (Carlisle, PA: Strategic Studies Institute, U.S. Army War College, 2011), 71.

CHAPTER 6

The first, the supreme, the most far-reaching act of judgment
that the statesman and commander have to make is to establish
by that test the kind of war on which they are embarking; neither
mistaking it for, nor trying to turn it into, something that is alien to
its nature.[1]

Introduction

This chapter examines the U.S. approach to counterinsurgency (COIN) in Iraq.

The U.S. entered Operation Iraqi Freedom in 2003 with a military that grew out of

Vietnam and envisioned the idea of a large, conventional force having the same success it

had during the first Gulf War. However, it was ill prepared for the fight that ensued after

the defeat of Saddam Hussein and taking control of Iraq. A campaign the U.S.

envisioned lasting six months ended up lasting eight years. The inability of the U.S.

civilian and military leadership to understand or admit what type of conditions had

emerged after the initial victory cost thousands of American lives. Quite simply, in the

words of one observer, "The force deployed to Iraq in 2003 had been too small to handle

the arduous tasks of occupation, internal security, and rebuilding."[2] U.S. forces did not

train for, were not prepared for, and did not understand how to transition from a combat

force to an occupying force. In addition, they were directed to build security forces and

assist in reconstructing a nation as a resistance movement developed and gained the

initiative.

---

[1] Carl Von Clausewitz, *On War* (New York: Random House, 1993), 100.
[2] Mockaitis, *Iraq and the Challenge of Counterinsurgency*, 1.

Thomas Ricks described the operational plan as consisting of "a few battles, not a plan to prevail and secure victory. Its incompleteness helped create the conditions for the difficult occupation that followed."[3] The U.S. intended to fight the type of war it wanted to fight based on years of preparation, doctrine, and training. It did not properly plan for what to do after the fall of the regime and the capture of Baghdad.

The insistence on fighting the type of war we wanted to fight and winning the first and decisive battle was a result of our Vietnam experience. After Vietnam, the U.S, military concentrated on bridging the existing doctrinal operational gap. The primary focus was winning the battle, not the war. The problem was the military did not know what to do once the battle was won. This new focus is evident in the following passage:

> "In learning how to be more operational," Scales said, "the Army may
> have lost its hold on both the higher, strategic lessons of generals such as
> Eisenhower, as well as on the lower, tactical lessons of counterinsurgency
> that it had learned in Southeast Asia. The National Training Center's
> scope covered only the fighting-defeating the enemy force, not figuring
> out what would follow. The plan for the spring invasion of Iraq reflected
> that view of war, emphasizing what it would take to get to Baghdad with
> little regard for what would follow. It was an operational plan,
> strategically deficient."[4]

Another result of the doctrinal revamp of post-Vietnam was that the U.S. Army "threw away virtually everything it had learned there, slowly and painfully, about how to wage a counterinsurgency campaign."[5] The American Way of War guaranteed a quick victory over Saddam's conventional forces, but did not provide a way to win against an insurgency. The U.S. military did not have the training or the doctrine required to fight a COIN in Iraq.

---

[3] Thomas E. Ricks, *Fiasco* (New York: Penguin Group, 2006), 115.
[4] Ibid., 132.
[5] Ibid., 133.

The Realization

Saddam's defeat and the capture of Baghdad went according to plan and major combat operations were over on May 1, 2003 when President Bush declared 'mission accomplished.' Unfortunately, this was not the end but the beginning of what became an eight year COIN campaign that the U.S. was not prepared for. The initial combat success and victory quickly turned to insurrectionist violence and insurgency against U.S. forces as many Iraqis saw the U.S. as occupiers, not liberators. Although Iraq was slowly slipping into an insurgency, U.S. Secretary of Defense Donald Rumsfeld refused to accept the new reality. On June 30, 2003 at a press conference, he told reporters, "I guess the reason I don't use the phrase 'guerilla war' is because there isn't one, and it would be a misunderstanding and a miscommunication to you and the people of the country and the world."[6] This party line was conveyed by all political and military leadership during the first months of the war.

The real catalyst for the development of a full blown insurgency was ironically caused by the United States with the arrival of Paul Bremer, the Coalition Provisional Authority (CPA). His first action was the total De-Baathification of Iraq society with CPA Order Number One, which purged the Iraqi society of Saddam loyalists. This led to tens of thousands of unemployed people who were previously running the government of Iraq. His next action and the most harmful to the Iraqis was CPA Order Number Two, Dissolution of Iraq Entities. This formally did away with the Iraqi armed forces, Iraqi police and security forces, and the presidential security forces. These actions ran counter to what the U.S. military intended for securing Iraq. Initially, the U.S. wanted to vet and

---

[6] Colonel Thomas X. Hammes, *The Sling and The Stone* (St. Paul, MN: Zenith Press, 2004), 173.

reform the Iraqi military and security forces. These actions fueled the fledgling insurgency into a full blown insurgency as moderates moved to support the insurgents against the U.S. occupiers. As one U.S. service member observed "When Bremer did that, the insurgency went crazy. May was the turning point" for the U.S. occupation, he said later. "When they disbanded the military, and announced we were occupiers-that was it. Every moderate, every person that had leaned toward us was furious."[7]

The realization and admission that the U.S. faced an insurgency in Iraq finally came on July 16, 2003 when General John Abizaid became the commander of U.S. Central Command. He stated that opponents of U.S. presence "are conducting what I would describe as a classical guerilla-type campaign against us."[8] The problem facing the military was how it was going to wage a COIN campaign since there was no supporting COIN strategy nor was there any doctrine to support this type of warfare.

2003: The First Year

The U.S. found itself fighting an unconventional war it was not prepared for. There was no coherent COIN strategy that guided U.S efforts during the immediate year after the fall of Saddam. With a lack of clear strategy or doctrine to inform the mission and purpose, U.S. forces leaned on what they knew best, conventional war. This conventional war approach, overreliance on firepower, and reliance on killing and capturing insurgents did little to advance U.S COIN efforts and actually made the situation worse. The approach taken at the beginning of Iraq is exactly what occurred during Vietnam. The lessons of Vietnam, our relegation of COIN to Special Operations

---

[7] Ricks, *Fiasco*, 164.
[8] Hammes, *The Sling and The Stone*, 174.

Forces (SOF), the over reliance on our conventional war mindset, and the lack of a coherent COIN strategy caused the early failures of the U.S. COIN effort in Iraq.

Moving Forward

As the insurgency continued to gain support, sectarian violence also began to spread throughout Iraq. As this occurred, there were operational and tactical adaptations made by soldiers who rediscovered effective COIN tactics. However, the lack of a comprehensive strategy limited the effectiveness of operational and tactical improvements.[9] In late 2005, the MNF-I commander, General Casey, commissioned a strategy working group to produce a report on best COIN practices. This report appeared in *Military Review* and listed the successful practices as: emphasis on intelligence; winning trust of the local population through protecting them and meeting their needs; unity of effort; an amnesty program for former insurgents; and moving the police to the fore in the COIN campaign.[10] These best practices are exactly how the British succeeded in Malaya and are the lessons that the U.S. should have applied in Vietnam. If the U.S. had chosen not to forget the negative COIN lessons from Vietnam and relegated this unconventional concept to SOF, the Iraq War might have turned out differently. Unfortunately, because U.S. military leadership chose to ignore COIN and invest no education or training in this very difficult operation, the vast majority of U.S. forces had no idea what a COIN operation entailed, nor did senior military leadership understand how to devise and implement operations that supported a COIN strategy. Because of the relegation of COIN outside conventional doctrine, it took U.S. forces two more years of

---

[9] Mockaitis, *Iraq and the Challenge of Counterinsurgency*, 125.
[10] Ibid., 132.

continuous learning and adaptation, trial and error, successes and failures before an attempt at a strategy was made to link nation building with COIN.

2006: The Supposed Answer

During the first three years of the Iraq War, U.S. forces waged a tactical COIN campaign based on the wrong application of British COIN efforts in Malaya, and a return to the *Small Wars Manual* approach. In 2006, the Department of Defense leadership heralded the arrival of FM 3-24, the new COIN manual for the U.S. military as the answer to the COIN problem in Iraq. It was an "impressive compendium of theoretical knowledge, historical examples, and practical advice"[11] but it suffered from the same myopia that crippled the U.S. efforts in Vietnam. It was strategic nation building tied to tactical COIN.

FM 3-24 took a combination of British and French approaches to COIN, and presented a tactical COIN approach that could apply to a large conventional force. The writers failed to realize that the British and French approaches were in response to colonial unrest, where they controlled all the means of power in the colony; the U.S. was in the midst of nation building and the colonial advantages did not exist. Thus, the tactics that had proven effective had little application in Iraq. Large conventional units applying tactical COIN was not going to succeed.

Conclusion

U.S. COIN in Iraq was a bottom-up, tactically driven, trial and error approach that lacked sufficient doctrine and a coherent COIN strategy to support a nation building strategy. FM 3-24 did little to explain how to conduct a COIN campaign. Once again,

---

[11] Ibid., 133.

the U.S. failed to learn from the historical lessons of the past and did not properly identify or plan for the type of war it faced. However, in Iraq, unlike Vietnam, the U.S. had only an insurgency to fight while nation building. The outcome in Iraq resembled the outcome in Vietnam: an Abrams-like approach to pacification and development of indigenous conventional forces. The resultant outcomes were also similar: a lack of U.S. strategic success. The following chapter examines the U.S. COIN approach in Afghanistan.

CHAPTER 7

Introduction

The U.S. entered Afghanistan with the focus of defeating Al-Qaeda (AQ) and its Taliban supporters enough to prevent any further attacks against the U.S. homeland. By the spring of 2002, a U.S. backed offensive utilizing Special Operations Forces (SOF) with the non-Pashtun tribes of the Northern Alliance successfully toppled the Taliban regime and installed a new government under Hamid Karzai. Operation Anaconda in March 2002 drove a significant number of hardcore AQ and Taliban fighters into Pakistan's Northwest frontier, allowing the U.S. a strategic opportunity to hand over primary security responsibilities to the NATO-led International Stabilization Forces (ISAF). The U.S. was not prepared to commit a large number of troops to Afghanistan as it was preparing for the invasion of Iraq. ISAF secured Kabul, but could do little more for the security of the remainder of Afghanistan; thus, an insurgency started to develop that ISAF continues to fight today.

This chapter examines the U.S. counterinsurgency (COIN) approach in Afghanistan. It reviews the insurgency, discusses early COIN tactics and approaches, and finally examines the most current U.S. approach to COIN. It also introduces its newest initiative to establish Village Stability Operations and the formation of the Afghan local police.

The Insurgency

The security situation in Afghanistan seemed to stabilize as the Taliban retreated into the Northwest Frontier to regroup, recruit, and train. This quickly ended in 2003 as the Taliban reemerged in Afghanistan, forcing ISAF to develop a COIN strategy that involved all nongovernmental and international agencies engaging in development and capacity building, but placed little emphasis on separating the population from the insurgents. The insurgency continued to grow over the next few years at the expense of the population, with the Taliban maintaining power through fear and violence against the population. The U.S. employed conventional forces in the same way it did in Iraq, employing Vietnam-style helicopter assaults coupled with heavy firepower to sweep villages and contested areas. While these operations often created a satisfying body count, they provided little help to the population. The insurgency grew and U.S. casualties mounted, to a point where lacking doctrine for COIN, a new approach was developed to deal with the insurgency.

The Early Approach – 'Clear'

In response to the growing insurgency, the U.S. deployed Provincial Reconstruction Teams (PRTs) as an approach to help establish limited security and respond to the needs of the population, a tactical approach first used in Vietnam before 1965. At the same time in 2003, LT General David Barno, Commander, Military Operations-Afghanistan began to experiment with deploying U.S. SOF personnel into local villages to live alongside the locals to gain their trust and cooperation, and to provide some security from the Taliban. This was an early pre-cursor to the now popular Village Stability Operations which this thesis discusses later in this chapter. These initiatives closely resemble the successful, but not ever fully executed, Combined Action Program of Vietnam.

U.S. SOF began to employ a tactical COIN approach similar to what had been done in El Salvador, other SOF forces executed a counterterrorism approach to kill or capture Taliban leadership, and U.S. forces began training Afghan security forces. Unfortunately, the U.S. did not sufficiently finance or properly man these due to the war in Iraq. Severely disjointed efforts that comprised a few tactical and operational successes failed due to the lack of a coherent COIN strategy built around the idea that we could just 'clear' our way to victory in Afghanistan.

The Way Ahead – 'Clear and Hold'

In 2009, the U.S. announced a surge of 30,000 forces to Afghanistan. In addition, 2009 was the year General Stanley McChrystal, the new ISAF commander, released a COIN strategy. This strategy fused all nation building and stability efforts from the district and provincial levels through to the national government. The strategy was based on regaining the trust of the Afghan people starting at the village level by establishing security and stability. Afghan villagers could defend themselves, resist Taliban oppression, and regain the normal life they desired. The new strategy also greatly increased the production and training of Afghan security forces, both the military and the police. This new population-centric COIN approach strived to:

> separate the insurgents from the population and increase the human security dimension-personal security, health and education, access to resources, governance, and economic opportunity. A population-centric approach aims to transform the environment and deny the Taliban the opportunity to erode the population's sense of well-being in the societal, governmental, and economic spheres of national activity.[1]

The current bottom-up COIN strategy is the first truly comprehensive and coherent strategy the U.S. had in Afghanistan. The new strategy took hold throughout the country

---

[1] LT General David W. Barno and Colonel John K. Wood, "Winning in Afghanistan," In *Counterinsurgency Leadership in Afghanistan, Iraq, and Beyond* (Quantico, VA: Marine Corps University Press, 2011), 115.

and showed positive results as security was established at the village level and Afghans were able to defend their villages and families.

Village Stability Operations

The new COIN strategy is founded at the village level. U.S. SOF conducts this mission through the Village Stability Operations (VSO) program to help develop the Afghan Local Police (ALP). This bottom-up COIN approach was highly successful and meets the most basic tenet of COIN which is to protect and secure the population. It also focuses on the center of gravity for Afghanistan which is the population. The overall goal of the VSO/ALP program is building the capability and capacity of village and district level officials through security to promote governance and development.[2]

The U.S. conducted the program in four phases: shape, hold, build, and transition. Modeled after the colonial French 'oil spot' tactic, VSO uses a 'conditions-based approach' to conduct operations by small units who have a decentralized chain of command at the local level. These operations are the classic COIN tactics used by the British and French that the U.S. ignored and overlooked for many years. It proved to be highly successful as it produced over 25,000 security forces that are now able to connect the village to the national government in all areas of security, governance, and development.

Conclusion

The U.S. strategy in Afghanistan evolved from denying safe haven, to 'clear', and finally to 'clear and hold.' Afghanistan is a war marked by tactical and operational

---

[2] Headquarters, Combined Joint Special Operations Task Force - Afghanistan, *Village Stability Operations and Afghan Local Police*, (Bagram Airbase, Afghanistan, April 01 2011), 7.

successes with very little to show in the way of an 'exit strategy.' This all changed in 2009 when the U.S. realized that it needed a comprehensive and coherent COIN strategy in order for the U.S. to one day withdraw from Afghanistan. It took seven years for the U.S. political and military leadership to realize that the true center of gravity for Afghanistan is the security of its people. All success in Afghanistan starts at the lowest level and when combined with an overall strategy, village and low level tactical actions have a strategic effect. Brigadier General Scott Miller, the commander of the Combined Special Operations Component Command gave his assessment in 2011:

> More than ever, there is a need for senior leadership to have a full understanding for actions at the lowest levels and it is also important for teams on the ground to fully understand the national level objectives and political situation. It may sound trite, but tactical actions are ever increasingly having strategic level effects. [3]

The current U.S. COIN strategy in Afghanistan is showing positive results. The security situation is increasingly better and the Afghan National Security Forces are performing at the required levels. The linkage of tactical and operational applications of COIN to a fully comprehensive and coherent COIN strategy is the reason for this success.

---

[3] Combined Joint Special Operations Task Force - Afghanistan, *Village Stability Operations and Afghan Local Police*, 1.

CHAPTER 8

The Future of U.S. Counterinsurgency

A large, conventional, firepower reliant military doctrine that seeks victory through fighting conventional wars hindered the U.S. approach to counterinsurgency (COIN) since Vietnam. The U.S. consistently failed to recognize it was fighting an insurgency and instead tried to fight the American Way of War. This approach did not succeed in Vietnam, Iraq, or Afghanistan and cost a great many lives and larger amounts of money.

In Vietnam, the U.S. had some initial success with COIN through the Civilian Irregular Defense Groups and the Combined Action Program. However, due to the conventional mindset of the military leadership, these programs gave way to the search and destroy approach that did little to secure the people. It was not until late in the war that the U.S. realized the need for a COIN approach that focused on a stability and nation building strategy but, by then, it was too late. Although the U.S. did develop successful COIN tactics during Vietnam, the inability to develop an overall COIN campaign properly linked to a COIN strategy that supported nation building led to the U.S. failure.

COIN has been described as "one of the casualties of the Vietnam War. After the debacle in Southeast Asia, the Pentagon wanted nothing to do with it."[1] The Department of Defense relegated COIN to Special Operations Forces (SOF) because of the disdain it had for these operations. SOF was instrumental in performing the tasks of COIN during the interwar years of post-Vietnam. COIN took on a new lexicon known as Foreign

---

[1] Thomas R. Mockaitis "Trends In American Counterinsurgency," in *The Routledge Handbook of Insurgency and Counterinsurgency,* ed. Paul B. Rich and Isabelle Duyvesteyn (New York: Routledge, 2012), 257.

Internal Defense during these years and was embraced by SOF as the new approach to U.S. COIN strategy. SOF conducted FID very successfully through these years with outstanding strategic results. It was the relegation of COIN to SOF that left the vast majority of regular forces unprepared for understanding or dealing with an insurgency that U.S. forces faced on the Global War on Terrorism battlefield.

In Iraq and Afghanistan, U.S. forces did not train for, were not prepared for, and did not understand how to fight a COIN campaign. The avoidance of COIN by the conventional military after Vietnam and the relegation of COIN to SOF left the U.S. military ill-prepared for the fight it faced in these two countries. Unfortunately, just as in Vietnam, the U.S. could not kill its way to victory through its preferred conventional war tactics. It had to fight an unconventional war in order to achieve victory. The central issue facing the U.S. was the lack of doctrinal understanding of COIN and how to develop a COIN campaign that properly linked the tactical, operational, and strategic applications to a comprehensive and coherent COIN strategy that supported a national strategy. John Nagl observed:

> These failures did not occur because the United States did not kill enough insurgents in these conflicts; they occurred because the United States and its allies failed to pursue coordinated, well-resourced counterinsurgency campaigns aimed at separating the militants from the population and strengthening the legitimacy of the Iraqi and Afghan governments. [2]

Fortunately, U.S. forces were able to gain enough tactical and operational successes in Iraq allowing the U.S. to withdraw without having a clearly articulated COIN strategy. In Afghanistan, there is now a COIN campaign that properly links the tactical, operational, and strategic applications of COIN into an overall COIN strategy. It is

---

[2] John A. Nagl, "Learning and Adapting to Win." *Joint Forces Quarterly*, issue 58, 3rd quarter 2010, 123.

ongoing and has great possibility for success and victory. The question that remains is the same one that plagued the U.S. in Vietnam: is it too little, too late?

This thesis states multiple times that no two insurgencies are the same. The lack of understanding about this fundamental idea of COIN by U.S. leadership greatly impacted its ability to design a COIN campaign, much less develop a coherent COIN strategy. In the past, the inability of the U.S. military to conduct COIN was a direct reflection of our preference for fighting conventional wars. The COIN experiences in Iraq and Afghanistan gained by the conventional military likely will follow the path of prior U.S. COIN experiences and be forgotten or pushed aside as the conventional force returns to its priorities. As the U.S. enters the post-war years of Iraq and Afghanistan, the Department of Defense (DoD) faces a fiscally constrained defense budget that requires shaping Joint Force 2020 to meet these budgetary constraints and be prepared to face the global challenges of tomorrow. DoD recently decided that future U.S. military forces will not be sized nor trained to conduct long-term stability or COIN operations. However, the Department of Defense needs COIN-trained forces now more than ever in the current fight against a global insurgency. The new global insurgency struggle is a long fight that requires small, highly adaptable forces able to move quickly into a crisis area that is coupled with a larger force to assist with security and the civil-military aspects of COIN.

COIN is truly a thinking man's form of warfare and, due to this idea; Special Operations Forces represent the best option for the future of U.S. COIN. COIN is a SOF core mission task that all personnel train for and conduct. The flexibility of SOF is inherent in their mission set; however, their operational vision of SOF 2020, pushes them to operationally integrate with strategic partners and allies across the globe by sustaining a forward presence in order to quickly respond to a crisis or conflict.[3] The global insurgency fight requires small, highly trained forces that possess the cultural skills, language abilities, and the ability to operate across the operational and strategic spectrums. These forces have the capability to train indigenous forces one day, capture or kill high value targets the next day, and conduct a civil affairs medical clinic building project the following day. SOF allows the U.S. to have strategic impacts in highly contested areas worldwide with the 'less is better' approach that will be required in the future.

In addition to SOF's ability to quickly move into a crisis area and begin to conduct COIN operations from the start, there is a requirement for a larger conventional force once operations begin. The Department of Defense should direct the standup of a standing COIN trained and focused division that can quickly deploy into a crisis area after SOF in order to provide the manpower and resources required to assist in eliminating insurgent infrastructure and protecting the population. This hybrid combination of SOF and a dedicated COIN trained and focused force will aid in the establishment of a secure operational environment and serve as a bridge if a larger U.S. force is required.

Counterinsurgency must be planned for, trained for, and treated as a form of warfare. The lessons of Vietnam, Iraq, and Afghanistan provide a historical accounting of how not to fight a COIN. The amount of time and resources spent to train and prepare forces once a COIN began was great. Standing forces properly trained who understand

---

[3] U.S. Special Operations Command, *Special Operations Forces 2020: The Global SOF Network,* (Tampa, 2013).

how to apply the key tenets of COIN from the beginning will ultimately reduce the cost in the current fiscally constrained environment. These forces are the foundation that allows the U.S. to design a COIN campaign and develop what is missing since Vietnam: a comprehensive and coherent COIN strategy that links the tactical, operational, and strategic applications of COIN for success and victory.

BIBLIOGRAPHY

Arnold, James R. *Jungle of Snakes*. New York: Bloomsbury Press, 2009.

Beckett, Ian F.W. *Modern Insurgencies and Counter-Insurgencies*. New York: Routledge, 2001.

Birtle, Andrew J. *U.S. Army Counterinsurgency and Contingency Operations Doctrine 1942-1976*. Washington D.C.: Center of Military History, 2006.

Blaufarb, Douglas S. *The Counterinsurgency Era: U.S. Doctrine and Performance*. New York: The Free Press, 1977.

Bogart III, Adrian T. *One Valley at a Time*. Military Report, Hurlburt Filed, FL: Joint Special Operations University, 2006.

Casey, George W. *Strategic Reflections*. Washington D.C.: National Defense University Press, 2012.

Cassidy, Robert M. *Counterinsurgency and the Global War on Terror*. Westport, CT: Praeger Security International, 2006.

Celeski, Joseph D. *Operationalizing COIN*. Military Report, Hurlburt Field, FL: Joint Special Operations University, 2005.

Clausewitz, Carl Von. *On War*. New York: Alfred A. Knopf, 1993.

Combined Joint Special Operations Task Force-Afghanistan. *Village Stability and Afghan Local Police*. Military Publication, Bagram Airbase, Afghanistan: Combined Joint Special Operations Task Force-Afghanistan, 2011.

Dixon, Paul., ed. *The British Approach to Counterinsurgency*. New York: Palgrave Macmillan, 2012.

Galula, David. *Counterinsurgency Warfare*. Westport, CT: Praeger Security International, 1964.

Hammes, Colonel Thomas X. *The Sling and The Stone*. St. Paul, MN: Zenith Press, 2004.

Headquarters Department of the Army. *FM 3-24 Counterinsurgency*. Field Manual, Washington, D.C.: Headquarters Department of the Army, 2006.

Headquarters Department of the Army. *U.S. Army Counterinsurgency Forces*. Filed Manual, Washington, D.C.: Headquarters Department of the Army, 1963.

Joes, Anthony James. *Guerrilla Warfare.* Westport, CT: Greenwood Press, 1996.

Kilcullen, David. *Counterinsurgency.* New York: Oxford University Press, 2010.

Kitson, Frank. *Bunch of Five.* London: Faber and Faber, 1977.

Melshen, Paul. "Mapping Out a Counterinsurgency Campaign Plan: Critical
    Considerations in Counterinsurgency Campaigning." *Small Wars and
    Insurgencies*, 2007: 665-698.

Metz, Steven. *Learning From Iraq: Counterinsurgency in American Strategy.* Carlisle,
    PA: Strategic Studies Institute, U.S. Army War College, 2007.

Meyerle, Jerry, Megan Katt, and Jim Gavrilis. *On The Ground In Afghanistan.* Quantico,
    VA: Marine Corps University Press, 2012.

Mockaitis, Thomas R. *Iraq and the Challenge of Counterinsurgency.* Westport, CT:
    Praeger Security International, 2008.

Mockaitis, Thomas R. *Resolving Insurgencies.* Carlisle, PA: Strategic Studies Institute,
    U.S. Army War College, 2011.

Mumford, Andrew. *The Counter-Insurgency Myth.* New York : Routledge, 2012.

Nagl, John A. "Learning and Adapting to Win." *Joint Forces Quarterly*, 2010: 123-24.

Newsinger, John. *British Counterinsurgency.* Hampshire: Palgrave, 2002.

Porch, Douglas. *Counterinsurgency-Exposing the Myths of the New Way of War.* New
    York: Cambridge University Press, 2013.

Rich, Paul B.,and Isabelle Duyvesteyn, ed. *The Routledge Handbook of Insurgency and
    Counterinsurgency.* New York, Routledge, 2012.

Ricks, Thomas E. *Fiasco.* New York: Penguin Press, 2006.

Rid, Thomas, and Thomas Keaney, ed. *Understanding Counterinsurgency.* New York:
    Routledge, 2010.

Schlosser, Nicholas J., and James M. Caiella, ed. *Counterinsurgency Leadership in
    Afghanistan, Iraq, and Beyond.* Quantico, VA: Marine Corps University Press,
    2011.

Thompson, Sir Robert. *Make for the Hills.* London: Leo Cooper, 1989.

Tierney, John J. *Chasing Ghosts.* Dulles, VA: Potomac Books, 2006.

U.S. Joint Chiefs of Staff. *Counterinsurgency Operations JP 3-24.* Publication,
    Washington, D.C.: U.S. Joint Chiefs of Staff, 2009.

U.S. Joint Chiefs of Staff. *Department of Defense Dictionary of Military and Associated Terms JP 1-02.* Publication, Washingtonn, D.C.: U.S. Joint Chiefs of Staff, 2013.

U.S. Joint Chiefs of Staff. *Joint Operations JP 3-0.* Publication, Washington, D.C.: U.S. Joint Chiefs of Staff, 2011.

U.S. Joint Chiefs of Staff. *Special Operations JP 3-05.* Publication, Washington, D.C.: U.S. Joint Chiefs of Staff, 2011.

U.S. Special Operations Command Headquarters. *Special Operations Focres 2020: The Global SOF Network.* Tampa, FL: USSOCOM, 2013.

Williamson, Murray, ed. *Strategic Challenges for Counterinsurgency and the Global War on Terror.* Carlisle, PA: Strategic Studies Institute, U.S. Army War College, 2006.

Woodward, Bob. *State of Denial.* New York: Simon and Schuster, 2006.

VITA

Lieutenant Commander Scott King is from Montgomery, Alabama and enlisted in the United States Navy in March 1991. He graduated from Basic Underwater Demolition/SEAL training with Class 183.

In November 1992, he reported to SEAL Team TWO where he completed three deployments that supported multiple operations including: Operation RESTORE HOPE (Somalia); Operations PROVIDE PROMISE, SHARP GUARD and DENY FLIGHT for Joint Special Operations Task Force TWO at San Vito AB, Italy; and Operation JOINT GUARD in the former Republic of Yugoslavia.

In July 2000, LCDR King was commissioned through the Seaman to Admiral Program and reported to SEAL Team ONE, where he served as a SEAL Platoon Assistant Platoon Commander.

In November 2002, he reported to Special Boat Team TWENTY-TWO, where he served as a Riverine Troop Commander and Command Training Officer.

In November 2005, he reported to SEAL Team TEN and served as a SEAL Platoon Commander deployed in support of Operation IRAQI FREEDOM (OIF) assigned to Special Operations Task Force WEST. He then served as a SEAL Troop Commander deployed in support of OIF while assigned to Task Force 17. Upon return from Iraq, he first served as the SEAL Team TEN Operations Officer, after which he assumed the duties of SEAL Team TEN Executive Officer and deployed in support of Operation ENDURING FREEDOM as Deputy Commander, Special Operations Task Force SOUTHEAST in Tarin Kowt, Afghanistan.

www.ingramcontent.com/pod-product-compliance
Lightning Source LLC
Chambersburg PA
CBHW080339290526
45790CB00010B/3758